CHARLATAN

charlatan

poems

Steven Laird

RONSDALE PRESS

RONSDALE PRESS
3350 West 21st Avenue
Vancouver, B.C., Canada V6S 1G7
www.ronsdalepress.com

Typesetting: Julie Cochrane, in New Baskerville 11 pt on 13.5
Cover Design: Julie Cochrane
Cover Photo: Michaela Bartonova, "Charlatan"
Paper: Ancient Forest Friendly Rolland "Enviro" — 100% post-consumer
    waste, totally chlorine-free and acid-free

Ronsdale Press wishes to thank the Canada Council for the Arts, the Govern-
ment of Canada through the Book Publishing Industry Development Program
(BPIDP), and the Province of British Columbia through the British Columbia
Arts Council for their support of its publishing program.

Library and Archives Canada Cataloguing in Publication

Laird, Steven, 1951–
    Charlatan / Steven Laird.

Poems.
ISBN 1-55380-022-2

    I. Title.

PS8573.A38113C44 2005   C811'.6   C2004-906685-4

At Ronsdale Press we are committed to protecting the environment. To this
end we are working with Markets Initiative (www.oldgrowthfree.com) and
printers to phase out our use of paper produced from ancient forests. This
book is one step towards that goal.

Printed in Canada by AGMV Marquis, Quebec

CONTENTS

CON'S HILL

DICTION

THE CRUCIFIC HOUR

ACKNOWLEDGEMENTS

I would like to thank the editors of *The Fiddlehead, Grain, Descant, Event, The New Quarterly, Whetstone, Tidepool, Lichen, TickleAce, Yggdrasil,* and *Southern Ocean Review* for publishing some of these poems.

Thanks also to Milan, Mark and James (the "Collected Unconscious") for their enthusiasm and critiques; Ingrid, Ruth, Gwynn and Andrea for their support and faith in the book in its many previous still-births; and Carmine for his expert, if sometimes wrong-headed, advice.

Special thanks to Breanne and McKenzie for keeping me crooked, and of course to Cathy for setting me straight.

Ronsdale Press would also like to thank Michaela Barto-nova of the Czech Republic for granting permission to use her stunning image of the puppet Charlatan on the front cover. The puppet is carved out of lime wood and plays an important part in Michaela's puppet theatre, Tineola, which has toured successfully across Europe. The figure of Charla-tan derives from Hieronymus Bosch's painting *The Waywain.* The reason Charlatan is figured with a saw in his hand is that, in the 15th century, he was portrayed as helping people "who are lost in their mind" by opening their head and extracting the disruptive matter.

In memory of Terra Buchanan

Dedicated to my friends,

the "Collected Unconscious"

For Cathy, constantly

"Reality cannot be reduced to language. . . ."
— MICHELE LALONDE

CON'S HILL

—

We live on
a headlong hill-
side atop a
stand-up town

Con's Hill

You can read these hills in translation
but to capture the thrill of their speed
you must hold your walking stick against them
like this, and allow the squandered rain
to roll from their backs with gossip.

These hills are sly and playful
they reach under seas when the seas least expect it
they tickle the waves, they clown around
at night, at great *vitesse*
you can hear the pitter
of little foothills —

A con, all of it. Listen.
At first light a silt of conspiracy
slows them to a fraud.
Benders. Injurers. Deliberate.

You can murmur your lovely prayers from the book
of stones, but how can you trust a thing
that moves this slowly
and still moves?

Harbour Main

The lexicon of waves is filled
with the marks of whispers and deep pauses —

to learn the speech of waves
is to sound each one, fathom by fathom

Their accents deafen our doors — if only
we could lose our grammar

we might, in salted conversation,
have something to say

to them, to each other

Fewer's Lane

The woods opens
its carmine pages
and closes again

and in that moment
when dogwoods sigh
and savage birds
tear at the leaves

there is a glimpse
of a crime and the cliffs

and a sense of forgiveness
awaits your perfect
bird-like dive.

Furey's Hill

the wind, handwritten in loose cursive
is not cramped with commas at all

rolls lightly, lifts the gulls and the crows
in risers and curls, sweeps the woods
disturbing whole seasons with unserifed clarity

equal to the rush and dive
breathless, thinking nothing

Gallows Cove

Salt water. and faces dying
everywhere into forms of fish
                    – FRANK O'HARA

Off they go to throttle their vessels
out in the mouth of Harbour Main,
          while the salt air blows and the salt sea crumbles

serious boats (unlike the Portuguese,
witless and white) of handcut lumber.
          work is work and play is drink
          while the salt air blows and the salt sea crumbles

What happens now
in the empty waters?
          the salt air blows and the salt sea crumbles

Chapel's Cove

It'll snick you in the arse, this coming
of All Hallow's Eve:

The trees in their cages are rusting;
the lips of the sea have grown cyanotic.

The hills are bristling with October shivers
and a net of steel clouds scrapes and hardens the roads.

People are burning their boats —

Shaggy-maned ponies and knitted sheep
knot like mist from the cutover fields.

Alone at the crown of Con's Hill
an old kabbalist shuffles a deck of cards.

Sea Fog at Sunrise

In complicated breakers
a gull stems from a rock —

things take shape and give up shape
while I gather wood from the beach

and the gull
leaps
from its shape

Rain Dance

there has been no new water on earth
since water was first introduced

complex, elegant processes
of evaporation, condensation, absorption
execute water through its classic phases

rain, seed, thirst, man, sweat

what happens in the interphase
remains unclear

and unearthly

For Terra, Aged 23, Missing and Presumed Drowned August 10, 2002

Cuckhold's Cove, Newfoundland, September 26th At 7:27 A.M.
Saturday — Sky Clear
Empty your thoughts of thoughts — up here
the cliff is no metaphor, the cove no dream
there are reasons to be accurate — the secrets of love
and wealth depend on it.

Walk the edge of the cliff — up here
eighty-seven feet falling sheer to the sea
you are precarious, the cliff is sure —
you need to be exact now.

Plan letters to no one, the sea abandons
love letters, sends no hidden messages
speaks of nothing — eyeless, the sea
feels its way and falls away

and is strewn with wind, flat, suggesting
a walk on its surface (you must be exact).
You have a rope of various bloods
use it to keep your balance in artistic
ways: like your mother, learn to play
the black keys of pianos too;
like your father, coil your rope
on beaches and Javanese temple steps.

Stand up here with only a rope
and your feet standing squarely on the mantle of this island,
tilted thirty-four degrees northeast.

East Of Here It's Later (Somewhere It's Yesterday)
East of here, the sun appears
(an exact star) to rise from the far horizon of a tumbled sea
(as if you could somehow arrive at this round world's edge).

A breath and a heartbeat later
you want to sing, or pray, or somehow
mark the occasion of morning.

And yet, at this moment, east of the sun
an afternoon drags its shadows through
the narrow streets of Calcutta, and east
of India there's a full moon hung
in an evening dewdrop over Fuji.

All the hours spill out all at once
on a green plate, on the face of a clock,
and the planet (a raindrop on the minute-hand
of the old town hall clock) sweeps along
under its own skies, in and out
of shadows.

Yet you see a horizon, one second
of the planet's sweep away, and you watch,
as morning and your song cross the line.

You cannot sing all the notes at once.
There are no songs like that, are there?
You parcel them out, time them, and hope
their roundness holds them from spilling

holds them clear, exact, above
the horizon.

Reading the Harbour

The harbour is mute, but rich
in gestures you can read,
in small tides and currents

water stretched by the tonnage
of displaced vessels, moored
between skies and the mess on the bottom.

Read what you want — romance
or industry, a whiff of *film-noir*
chill and fog, a new atmosphere

that dampens your collar, the mystique
of ships on their ropes, under flags of convenience,
with a cargo of keys

bound down for Labrador —
but don't be fooled —
the seas have no purposes.

Be like that, and like the seas
be restless, timeless, and bound down
for no place special.

If Waves Were Horses

When so many seas run
no bottom so deep that
you haven't been there

and all you're handed
the money the time
the naïveté and the
inclination

isn't mountain enough
for your vertical prayers
who can you blame
that the tilt of this island
is to the northeast?

If north is stone and
east is the wind
who are you to be
so precise

If the sea is time
then drowning is the end
to restless rocks always
rolling and falling.

(This is important, it's
the label on the jar —
if it's smudged or in Latin
you don't spill it.)

If north is the rock
and the east is dawn
let the tilt affect you.
Let someone see you.

Shine, man, shine
like the toe of your boot.

Learn the ropes and
empty your pockets
of things
that will drag you down.

Floating Dock

It's the end of September, the end of the light
of day, enough to warm this floating
dock where you cool your tired heels.

The sea is empty, so's the sky
even the rocks are full of nothing
but long-standing gestures, and nothing's moving
everything's falling away.

There's just you and Sue, who's half your age
with twice your wit
      and seems to like you.
There's a bottle in a paper bag.
There's just this moment, no redemption
and no need for one, your salvage is at hand —
Sue passes the bottle and swears she never
looks behind her, and to hell with the cops,
and she leans back on a pile of old ropes.

There's no moment like this one, and you'll never know
or need to know how this island will lean,
where the moon will rise exactly, or when
the next ship leaves.

DICTION

—

a shill
a con
a carney barker

I'd Like to Know

Is it the quiet working of worm in earth
or the clear cut of axe in wood, spade
on rock, steel wheels on steel tracks
or the highway whining in the far night
or the soft tear of silk?

Is it animal muscle lengthening under
rubbed skin, or anodized iron freezing
the ribs of a bridge in the dark? Is it metallic
with the taste of blood or hot and generous
with the fat taste of marrow?

I'd like to know, beyond air and the occupation
of useful purposes (location in space, the order
of need and narration of sequence) how it really sounds
when the voice is no longer bound up
in earth, iron, ice, reason, alarm.

How Do You Say

How do you say
what can't be said?

teeth tongue tonsils palate
larynx lungs lips
"will" above all in the skull's cap
and a fish rib in the exit wound

How do you tell
what can't be counted?

with a shared tooth
("sum tymes bytin sum tymes bit")

how do you shout
whatever is silenced?

a sore tongue
splitting latched words

How do you sing
all the notes at once?

voice box squeezed
between the knees

How do you whisper
what can't be kept quiet?

breathe in breathe
out
the folds of a lung

How do you say
what can't be said?

scaling the fish bone
deep in the throat

If I Had an Accent

If I had an accent
things would be different

between us. Your interest would be piqued
I wouldn't have to speak

loudly to be heard
just slowly to be understood.

Your familiar English syllables
would wax and wane undecidedly

on my tongue like an unfamiliar view of the moon
rising and falling over rooftops at Kowloon.

My cadences would rock you slowly
the movement of stone over stone over time

and the off-rhyme, misplaced
and mispronounced, would make you want me

to speak over and over
the slow mesmerizing words of love —

all this and the true beat of my heart
if I had an accent, and yes, a scar!

Tambourine

There is a quiet at the tongue's root
where my begging bowl hangs on a wooden nail
where in my library of knives
silver thins the viscous blood
silver corrodes the iron blood
where in the dark I speak American Sign Language
where a robin's egg in a gymnasium
where the light of peated water and the light of bees
where all these whisper, and all these whispers
come to rest, come to rest
in a tambourine's emptiness

and gather to speak and will speak
voice of the liquid sun in Martinique
voice of oranges, voice of swung hammocks
voice of lazy water weighing half a sunken log
voice of dog and hair of the dog in the heat
voice of messages in air-mail blue sky from afar, afar
(come home by fastest), voice of dreams in the afternoon
in whispers that whisper
come to rest, come to rest
in a tambourine's emptiness

and work breath and spit to solvent, to loosen:
from hard wax, a grace of flame
from tough cane, a sweet prayer, a delight
from blood, a verb and a step ahead
from the brass foot of God, a boat to swim in the wind
from the kneeling gardens, from evening, a pool and a root
from the caves of gods, luminous moss
from rained cement, from wet summer sidewalks, a whisper
come to rest, come to rest
in a tambourine's emptiness

Sun

an act of saying
open
the turn of handles
    sun: a celestial body, a star

the act of saying,
sigh,
the open leaf and wing
    sundial: time by a shadow

the act of saying a psalm forever
along your thigh, a proverb along
your bare arm
    sunshade: a parasol

the act of saying —
your breast
under light cloth against my tongue
    sunburst: a sun surrounded by rays

the act of saying:
recite!
surrender, sunder
    sundisk: emblem of the sun

the act of saying
yes
without love, without lies
    sunbirds: resembling hummingbirds

the act of saying
shut
a crippled moon in a rigged tree
    sunstruck: touched by the sun

Ouidajanesi

Yes! the very smile of the word
　　　The assent of *s* the wide grin of *e*
　　　　　the mix of you and I in *y*

Yes! knows more than the perky *yep*
　　　Yes! more determined than lazy *yeah*
　　　　　Yes! with more heart than timid *uh-huh*

Let *Yes!* begin every contract and doubled
　　　Yes! and *Yes!* the end of dispute
　　　　　Yes! the promise of every vow

Yes! so easy to say and *Yes!*
　　　Is pleased and *Yes!* a hope made real
　　　　　Yes! Yes! Yes! as passion climbs the scale

Yes! enters laughing
　　　Yes! I do *Yes!* we can
　　　　　Yes! it's you *Yes!* he is

And *Yes!*
　　　I will!

Diction

from now on WATER
is a sentence a state of lifting
from ice to atmosphere

and TREE is a dictionary
the root of the single word
leave

GRASS is a hilarious paragraph
in the frightening *film noir* of fields

WIND therefore no longer means
air in motion
it is the cuff of large seas,
an anecdote of meadows

SPRING now refers
to a subtle shift
in the tension of lovers

Tremors

been such a long liedown
among the reedy boulders
        shoulders / shudders

all mouth so
hungry to talk

come the tremors,
heat before the
        eclipse / collapse

approaching
        encroaching / crouching
at the speed of thunder

and just before it hits
        at last, at last

will open its mouth
        swallow
        all your
        seas and cities again

for want of talk
for want of an equal voice
        listener / sinister / silent

:groan

Poetry Reading in a Disused Church

A chapel only wants to pray
rain and voices raised in hymns
are its delight

It's raining on the Great Lakes
and a chaplain wants to hold out
one good hope

It helps to know a hymn might break
the webs in rafters
gathered through the careless years

The Great Lakes and the rain are church enough
and hope unmeasured makes me
raise my voice

above the webs in roof-beams

Arabic

I — and I break my fist
against unburnable words

how the minutes stretch their legs and hours
walk immensely across the sun

afternoon-slow against drawn curtains
'Listen!' those eyes that shut all doors behind them

Give me shade and cold water
a room a word against my unslakeable fist

A Failure of Nerve

after Léon-Paul Fargue

one long brass-timbered oar glistens with dew, disarmed
a come-on sad as cinders, a tendency of branches
lay floored, and foils suppress a sound

the view over glass in the evening of evening in
the end surely packs a punch

      in a mason's mask
one soldier plays satin chords on a clarion
comes unravelled, dissolves the key, rejoins the horizon

the bark of night is ready to partake of
doves, indoor's a war's early chesterfield
averts once-laconic "no sir" applause

the low mirror rubble, succulent and tame, a
new lapel never illumined, no vision
no bloodclot no verdigris armor
no fencers

      unattended
a couple of strangers lounge around a rug, raise
their voices
      do vacant airs, undo
      treasures you plundered

one day's enough
two share a concern, two share a pardon, and
painters afraid of the forest's new valley
put attention in jeopardy

      we make new vows amid
our tenderness, but we kill our savvy promises

The Word Made Flesh

after Neruda

Bella
come in fresh-foot to the mansion
your elegant ankles rekindle
the pagoda of foam as the sunrise detours

Bella
the day finds many idols and spies
come into the plate cabinet and dance
on the floor of a world easy to view

Bella
a conundrum of cobras tangles you
enter the gazebo at night
colour the maelstrom bright as day
make the horizon hard, irrepressible

Bella
in the cabinet your eyes are lost in care
in the cabana your eyes are lost in tears

I pray as I ride into sorrows
my patriots stand in Tuscan ranks
your camisole revels
in lights and loose almond shells —
pardon this yoke of mine

Bella, my Bella
too fast too happy too soon
too sure too loose too sombre

Bella
today I marble quarried by surprise
when you can taste odours
when you can see fresh suns
        sigh and pray
when the west circles the east
        sigh and pray and erase me
I am liable
always

Script

He picks up the book
He puts the book down
There are no flies
The air is calm

He picks up the book
Turns it in his hands
It used to be a red book with a brown cover
But now it is a green book that used to be white
But now is yellow
And it has no cover

He puts the book down
Walks away
Stops, turns back, and

Picks up the book
Feels the Moroccan leather
That now no longer covers it
Flips the pages
Written in Cyrillic with Cantonese accents
And Arabic underlines
He puts the book down
Walks away

He is thinking about the book
Was there ever a book like it?
He wants to prise out its secrets
He wants something to show for it
He walks back to the book

Picks it up
Caresses the Sanskrit edging on its Hebraic pages
He is a sensualist and
There is no book
Like it
He holds it in two hands
Now in one hand, wing-clasped to his chest
He studies himself in the wineglass
With a professorial air
He imagines things about the book
And they become true
Everything about the book
Always comes true
He puts the book down

The book rests from its exertions
On a cherry wood table
It is a fine book indeed
Thousands of pages, thirty-four occurrences
Of the letter Z, an index
He walks away from the book

He picks up the book
And weeps
He puts the book down and
Laughs
He picks up the book
And is become death, the shatterer of worlds
He puts the book down and
Is hungry in a dead language

Whatever is he going to do about this book?
Is it his own? His mother's?
Did he find it in the subway or a mosque?
Was it written before the 12th century
Or just published then?
He does not know its provenance
He picks up the book and leaves the room

But is soon back with the book, places it carefully
On the rosewood table
Where again the book rests
Between its missing covers

He picks up the book
Several pages appear
To be missing

He leaves the room
Leaves the house
Steps out into the leaves
Of the fine October air

Charlatan

The secret to speaking, he said, and his
bone finger against her small mouth
and they boarded the circus train as the circus boarded
and sat with the conductor, his whistle and key
and took care that they did not disturb
the elephant, the monkey, and the man on stilts

and the green train shone through the wonder of hills
rising and falling through afternoon and its turns
on its way to the sea, Is the song underneath
does it come from the sky, from the ground, this matters
as she sang in the corner by the cabman and the sunlight
shrieked with the whistle of the train

the circus was happy the cabman shared his lunch, Speak
    well of the dead
we ought therefore to *allure their souls*
by spells that move them to harmony:
as are *voices, songs, sound, enchantments;*
as prayers, conjurations, exorcisms, and other rites,
as are, and here again her singing was full

their trip continued across the hills of various names
and still goes on, old man, granddaughter,
conductor and cabman, circus and sandwiches
and her voice clear as salt in the sea and on the rails
And remember they want entertainments to go
with your snake oil and leech cures

and only in song, she's never spoken
and he, old buzzard and once a prince among the ibises
writes in a grid struck by sunlight off the sea
through the green train's windows, with a saw,
his feathers dry and useless for this work
and she doesn't read and her heart is light as sawdust

GETTING A FIX

—

as contracted as a lawyer
exacting pound for pound
  a way to find a way to tip the scales

Thoughts while Running an Errand

How personal! How ordinary!
To walk inside your t-shirt
where the oldest street in the new world
avoids your reflection
(everything begins with an audience)

chain-smoking your way to the liquor store,
in the frames of your own movie

where young women stare at your jeans, knowingly
and young men meet with you to talk style —
you want the wind to pick up right on cue,
you want to mope beautifully
your right leg never still.

You could go on forever in this vein —
a vampire whose only moment in the sun
begins the tragedy, while the audience begins
to forget —

Oh anything, anything at all, to keep
this hour's light playing back and forth
on the white keys and their shadows — anything,

to keep your biographer intrigued
and the wine flowing — which reminds you
of your personal task —

change in your pocket
bottle of Bluebird
in a paper sack.

Slowly I Turn

slowly I turn
into a quiet lake

a woman swims deep
in an odd current

while at the other end a man
glides with skill across the ice

this is impossible
but it is the end

when sunlight is heavy
and the patterns of trees

are printed in sand
on the clear, empty bed

Slow River

It is night, I am working
the slow northern river,
working my boat among
star roots
in slow panes of river.

Above me, a river of air. I am calm.
My blood works. My thinking falls
like rivers, like nights pulled down
slowly by their star-filled weight,
my blade in their field

drawing single stars
Rigel, Aldebaran,
through sinking rills in the paddle's wake.

The starry element under my boat,
the slow river, determines my course.
I am bound by its bounds, work its workings.

Erosion

Hooded I kneel to a quiet stone
raised on a bouldered mountain apron
among sulphured stone and tumbled scree
raised from an old stone-age sea bed
among thin weed stalks and lichens lost
in stone, raised in scorch and ice
though nothing here stands higher than
the scouring wind

      my feet are cold
from walking in cloud, my knees crook'd
and sprung among the wasted stones
the cables of my bones are laid
with signals and messages, my hands fold
in a cloak, work secretly, sky and strong
sunlight corrode my eyes and my voice
a dried whisper scraped across
snowfields —

I pray slowly over uncertain hours
in clear light where it is hard to see
that I might turn to stone and live
that simply, that my reason might
become veins of quartz, my passion gold
my body magnetic, an island unanchored
to the mantled earth —

      hooded I rise
from my bones' complaint, move across
the planet's crust,
eroded, carrying
dust

Ilderton

No, the house has not fallen
Into smallness, the kind that occupies
Things while you take thirty years
To walk back to them. It's held

A tough grace against the gravel road,
And the farmed and carefully emptied fields,
And the long electric fence down to the schoolhouse.

None of these wide acres and years
And not the coming rains in the sky
Have reduced it or made
My excitement smaller.

The creek is no smaller than when I was five
And the ice was a clear window to the green
Reeds under it, waving in clean running water.

That mailbox named my father.

The yard is no smaller, and only the sky
Has fallen into low sweeping rains
(I remember the rain in that chestnut tree)

And only my heart has widened
In the occupation of walking back.

Typical

Is it the house that shakes
or the night that drums so late?
      – TESSA RANSFORD, *MEDUSA DOZEN*

It's the house.

It's the joists and stringers as they creak back into their empty
    shape —
they become less solid, lightening with each passing storm.

It's the hearth stones loosening — they become light as bread
with each feather of flame.

Last night as you tried to sleep I heard the roof,
the rafters as they dried, the shingles evaporating around our
    heads.

The walls have sprung leaves, and the eaves
curl and become brittle, about to fall.

It's the house as it tries (as all houses try in their witness
to the weary patterns of occupation and neglect)
to shake off the earth that undermines it.

It's the house as it tries to grow wings,
to take to the permanent sky and become
a fit habitation for the likes of you and me.

Highway 401

Trucks by the mighty come
sprung from the slots
rampant, impelled,
white hot and headlit
brakeless as the stitches
of white lines shroud by
       on Highway 401

Abandon fills the trailers
what's left of built,
assembled, harvest,
rend and cast-off
red-letter loud
with a name and a slogan
          and the rain comes down

   pavement by the tarload
   black-dogs the wheels
   and the wheels go on
   and the dogs let up
   there's no moon tonight
   but the road itself is
   so immense
       so still
         and the rain comes down
on Highway 401

From 60

Is it dark yet?
It's still dark.
Can I go now?
Keep going.
Where shall I go?
It's still dark, there's no one to see.
I have nowhere to go.
Keep going.
Who should I ask for?
It's still dark, you won't see anyone.
Where shall I find him?
Keep going.
How much time's left?
60. It's still dark.
Keep going.

False Map

We aim at simplicity and hope for truth.
– NELSON GOODMAN

The map you provided
I threw to the unmarked winds
as I sped through the morning sun.

The freeway I travel
is black, where you drew it in red.

There was no dotted line
halting through fields at the border.

When I drove through a town
imagine my unease to find
it was not, as you guessed,
a round black dot.

Clearly you've never been.
And surely you can't be relied on:

Today is a gorgeous spring day
and your map failed to turn
the lovely bright green of the fields.

Mind Body

If my foot had a brain it would welcome the mud.
– EPICTETUS

If it had its own way
the foot would be happy
on bare solid ground, stable, foretold
in every direction, capable and clever at
dancing.

If it had its own mind
the hand would be pleased
with a firm grasp and an instrument's touch
with its delicate sense of heat and ice
and differences.

With a mind of its own
what more would a back need:
the brace of the wind, the strength of the sun,
gravity.

But all these limbs
in their useful course
dangle in a rig from a mind with a mind
of its own
distracted, corrupted, daft with dreams
and haunted by uncertain outcomes.

PASSWORDS

—

Drumbelly burn he got
no dark places he
beatin out the shadows outta
everybody faces oh my
Drumbelly come

Atlas

I come a big man on a road of rock
no earth can bear the crush of my heel
I come a heavy step a king's stride a swagger
to rest whole skies on the roll of my shoulders

       a big man, bone-heavy, blatant with thrust
       of forward chest and steady gaze
       clear-eyed and monstrous with lust, a root
       in my hand, a trunk for a thigh, a landslide

I come a big man, carrier, dray
to the sun, hauling it lightly in orbit
around the morning, fat red sun
to burn the iron-tough skin of my back

       a big man, careless, thunder in every
       breath, that low-throated deep-ground rumble
       shakes your houses, wakes your nervous
       dogs, your willing, aching wives

I come a bristled man, bikered with beard
horned hands and sweat that runs like rain
from my brow, holding earth in my mouth
like a stone to keep me from raging thirst

       a big man, the weight and crush of planets
       such earth-heavy visions in your thickening dreams
       rained on and windblown, sunburnt and driven
       nothing and no one stands in my way

I take what I need, joyous and wild
I have no master, no book, no house
can hold me, no dream too large to stop
my restless step on this road of rock

      a big man a grown man a child a beast
      of burden an earth-mover sky-shaker sea-troubler
      I come a big man a belly a buddha
      the sky is my shadow, I lighten the earth

Blondin

All the trains
       shunt, muscle and lumber
bells toot and whistles ring

And the trucks
       strut their bright red coxcombs
shift to high and rumble

While the cars
       scurry and bristle they
scoot and flip the bird
       to the flashing sun

And the buses
       oh the buses!
hum from hive to hive
       and the buzz of the high white cloud

The old road
       knuckled and distracted
fills with flapping crowds *and*
tons of river wing over the lip

Oh Niagara!
       your harmonica wires!
Blondin is crossing the
       Falls again

Banshee

for Lucy

I am wild rain in a bird's body
I am wind under wing, a rustle in the hedges

I am a hive of lightning on a lake
a gale of howls, a ruffled feather

a shivered keening in the dead cold night
a nail loose in the coffin, nine inches deep

I am the stone at the top of the hill
I am the rolling of holy ground

listen to me but do not listen lightly
for I am a poet, madwoman, a thunder

and I will surely take you under

The Pull of Magnets

I moved or the earth
crested its lithic wave
in an undertow of rock

claustral caves or my eyes
opened, the day sky flew off
to the stars and I lay with the planet

alert: your breath or the wind
changed pitch, a door closed, a star set
the pull of magnets relented

between us hearts or the earth
drummed, shifting continents apart

Riches

While nights rained, lost and falling
in the tossed glint of gemstones,
we came together out of rain in remembrance
to greet her one final time.

A small handful of solemn hearts
of salt, empty and burning —
three pews in twenty braced the mourners
pressed among echoes and a few wreaths.

And leaded closed, a stone coffin
deaf, solid and secret
in the hard, gold light, a chrysalis
for the frail ghost of her body.

With a last prayer the pastor ended
a lesson. We all passed on,
she to sea-bright shoals in the sun,
we to read shells half-buried in sand.

Antaeus

for Lesley

she walks the rails, and with each hard step
of boot on cinder, a seam of coal
burns in her heart, and hot gold in her blood

and with each steel mile her bones become
iron in leather, with a touch of silver
in each wired nerve

she gathers stone and strength of timber
creosote under her fingernails
leaf mold in her kiss

and she goes to ground, unshakeable
but for the rumbling of the freight train coming
from somewhere underground

and she's coming for you

A Rose in Your Teeth

if you really loved me
your accordion might be red
your dress might flicker
and your hat might be tilted
in a jaunty way, between wild rhinos
on the esplanade

and if you really loved me
there might not be so many horns
horns in the cookies you bake
horns of plenty when I'm out of town
antlers in the tub, so hard to take
a shower or a bath

if you really loved me
you might have asked about the river
saying "is this a river?"
without your usual capital letters

and if you really loved me
out of all the other club-hoofed birds
there might at least have been
a rose in your teeth

Removing Shoes before Mosque

your skin, your wheat and olive,
unassumed, I avoid your eyes
> *you have what I want*
> *without faces*

at your door I bend
remove my shoes
> *when does He put*
> *balance in the knee?*
> *the knee that rescues you?*

I am announced a stranger
common as gravel, overbearing
> *ask about me?*
> *ask a stone coming from a hill*

I have prayed for this
hours of burnt words
> on winds,
you are my messenger

these are borrowed clothes
a good fit
they will be gone tomorrow
> *oh weapon mine*
> *oh expensive loss*

> *you have what I want*
> *without faces*

The Accountant

sun blades
slanting through a blind
mark pencil lines in the lifting steam
of her coffee

desk trays
sheets of ledger paper
loosen this light in pale rectangles
of scatter

she is the resistance
armed with mechanical pencil
clips slide rule hand-held calculator
she graces

Arabic numerals
through columns of the infidel
her pencil has no eraser, she takes
no prisoners

hers is not
to win but to find the right balance:
in a fence of books, a vase loosens petals
of geraniums

Gazelle

I read clarities
drawn in water over her skin

I cross myself —
a flag against the wind

How many centuries have gathered dust
together to make me vain?

My sanity, a blade against a grindstone
this madness, the rains

I open my map case —
strange birds fly in!

Satisfied with the love of her —
and never satisfied

I walk in old sunlight at dusk
casting off the long shadow of sleep

She brings the most innocent present:
a single flower to the greenhouse keeper

Outer Cove

just out from the beach, smooth round stones under her foot,
    the tide evening out
(with all of her a perfect secret to me, I can only watch),
black dress hiked in one hand to her knee, barely ankle deep
    but commanding the wind
blown out from Ireland by the law of storms to rise through
    her hair (how my fingers ache)
just so she can say she stood there, then, in the sea, and drank
    rum to the dregs like any
crazy fisherman — an act only she understands in her african
    heart, through her bare feet,
in the complex, slow, private wash of the waves, by the hot
    light of the burnt sun —
(later, after the thunder, the moon will rise as simply as that,
    and as eternally)

sweet jasmine in earth in a clay pot on the sill, this clean scent from
    the earth
in the clay pot, some rain blows in over the sill, and this scent of
    clean
rain over jasmine, rain on the clay, sweet rain on the wind, blows in

THE CRUCIFIC HOUR

and other times

The Crucific Hour

This morning, while the sun seeded the daisies,
while gold atoms scattered in eddies
and the earth hid its age among flowers
and the sun gilded the house like a jar of honey
you unearthed my stonecutter's heart.

In the arc of your body
I only wanted to leave tangible gestures.
When we flew, we longed for roots;
I only wanted to be air in the air.
When we flew, we longed for rough dust.

I was a navigator in the tumult of your body
I rang like a bell tower rocked by the wind
I rang like old and punished bronzes.

Backing down the ragged ways
we shone, and still longed for each outbreak of rust.
We loved fatigue with a secret restlessness
and ignored everything generously.

You were the one that found God in the aromas
of savage perfumes.

After, the gore of lightning
nailed the prairie like a gold lance;
after, it rained knives, and left deep wounds in the moon;
after, begging in a locksmith's shop,
lodged in the exact place of our errors,

your mature and offered heart,
like salt flowers, opened with a glance.

Under the Terms of Wear

You said to me if you write to me
do not type.
Any joy has its defect.

I cannot regain the evening anymore:
in the room, only despair does not have wings.

The inderacinable feeling of love:
it is a sifted boat of snow, if you want,
like birds that fall and their blood does not have
the least thickness,

and its circle of beauty
always bites the tail:
the drudgery of trees will still make a forest.

The air of the room is beautiful like drums,
the clouds run on the ignited moon, a jewel of hair,
in the evening, at the seaside, when the stars *chantonnent*.

All that I say to you comes of a wild selfishness
and I do not understand the language
of your whispering churches.

These recent marks announce
the powerful step and claws of two large wolves

moving all the categories of the human spirit
in all directions,
without knowing its difficult mechanics.

An Ebb Tide I Hum of Anaesthesia

In the immense blond calm of the afternoon
sung to sleep at the bottom of distant conversations
the serpent coiled in her throat.

As if she walked furrowing a wheat field in seed
yes, as if furrowing a sea of crossings
with porcelain wings and the sweet blade
of the cargo and the company.

As if with the starting of trains
they took innumerable daisies to her.
As if they took the blue days to her,

the secrets of the wind
where the old shades go
by caves of wolves and vixens,
past strange flowers, between the rubbish of castles
and by humble water that becomes
the prey of the mill.

Love is a word
that in wanting, takes shape.

All Deaths Are Drunk of Old and Cold Rain

I dreamed of you, your profile on my throat
you whose mouth is made with several tongues:
my heart beat like a shutter.

I take a thousand precautions not to shock my wife
I am the ridiculous amateur in the medium of professionals.

One day a star will die out and the rivers become calm,
I will be rich with two goblets
and I will marry the girl from the vineyard.

I can distinguish clearly the white thread:
dreams startle at the calamity of birds as dawn approaches.
The moons and the centuries will pass
and always the same idiotic hour returns.

Ah, to kill it perfectly.

Sixty steps on a limited road
in praise of widows — as you leave
to be with your Turkish lover
do not write my name on the ground.

From Summer, from Winter,
from Meanwhile, in So Short a World

She dreamed a Greek merchant in a certain region made
    traffic.
(Contracts are the door by which noise entered the world.)
Our Greek himself went everywhere plaintiff.

She dreamed:
the attentive one charged her with a message for Mahomet
right in his paradise.

She dreamed when the wolves delivered engagements.
Dreamed two demons with their liking shared our life
and of her inheritance drove out reason.
She returned thanks to the sky of the happy adventure.

She dreamed: one cavils, one causes indicters
to burden people by their stops.

Dreamed: I will count them in vain
they were more than a thousand.

She dreamed heads, multitudes, and to the least lamb
delivered entreaties to hold firm.

She dreamed what the sky wanted to put out of space.
Dreamed her heart became the goal of all the features
that love launched.

It is the heart alone which can make quiet.

A Smooth Air, of Slow Turns

(dawn)
By one of those rare reflections of the light
that physicists fill books with formulas to explain
the dawn flatters your hands with its fugitive wing
and the wind aspires.

Your hands, slight as fire,
in the gesture of wounded birds,
your body light as a boat run aground
in the confines of my look,

your tired and wise hands —
gold dreamed on the skin.

(afternoon)
The cardinal-red afternoon hours:
it was in a smiling garden, the calm source of crystal.

He was brave, he was beautiful, she was artist
elegant and discreet assassin, sent
from the prince of the seven suns.

I know the strange names of grass and its seeds
and mortal conceit and sublime pains
and a thousand names of women
and a thousand leaves of jasmine, shelled and light

your marginal caresses
which come and prick the grain from my palms.

(twilight)
The lion dreams
next to the three palms;
the sun is tamed.

In the sand, the clastic shade
shakes with tigers.

(midnight)
Poetry is a loaded mercury weapon
I make braids of verses, mess your hair

I keep between my treasures of sanity
a lucent mirror and a nostalgia for madness
I do not want to be immune
to the emptiness of many days without desire
and burrow in the wet bitter taste

your paper boat drowned in the rain:
a thousand flowers unclasp
these thick patient hands.

The Insufficient Echo of Human Transit

I came down among the uncultivated fields
to walk the evening long in the blue eclipse
of the river, the meander to which the sky twists
its sadness, and its corners of fire.

(From the earth, iron and coal, a generated fire
raises its splendid question marks from high stacks.)

In the evening hour conspiracies
the time between the sluices of the river slides
and small sails waken some timid sirocco
(who coils a fresh wind when the hurricane is past?)

I arrive where I am foreign, in the garden of Gulhané
with my imperfect tenses, among unknown vines
with only my belief in burnt notes to lovers,
in the precision of gestures, in the eccentric orbits
of fingers.

It will snow in the hills in a few days, the bushes
will fold under the weight of answers.

Gulhané: garden and zoo in Istanbul

Qarin

Compare me to a dry marsh near Kafr El Sheikh,
out of the empty hum of light, the rush of your wing across
    reeds.

With many languages cut into your skin, you settle on me,
you crane your neck above me, you murmur insanely.

The shells of your words rattle me,
the shadow of your skin moves constantly against mine.

I resemble the desert river, bent through Edfu, El Kab, Esna,
as if I'd forgotten the great fall of water at the source.

The wind from your hair shivers skin and surface,
you lean back above me, the sun leans a garden of light
    across your heart.

It is as though at El Qahera all the choked water gives way.
Here is where the moon fills; here my voice is paper.

You startle, and lift your heated blood from the bank of my
    body
I am left under blank lightning; dry seeds sink in the White
    Sea at Alexandria.

Second Dangerous Flight

When I crossed the large and terrible skies
she awaited me in a great angle of shade —

her festival of sex, a collision of panic and fury
with the most alive silver, a mineral fire.

Her hands full of desire, dark ecstasies of black wine,
her pearls are stars over the night of her skin.

She writes her burning name with ivory and tar,
in drops of money, in the risky language of goldsmiths.

She is in love with the day's transparency,
its cane lullaby, the wind in the air,

the sea on the reef,
and the slowness of the sun —

so many beautiful sounded hours,
as autumn is thinned out of leaves.

As for me, that same obstinate syllable of blood
became a gleaming blade, a wire, a single and vain rail.

Macbeth Appears on the Naked Platform Covering His Sex with His Hands

Her magnificent animal and amazon complexities of
    bowstring and breast:
the hour of the tooth, the "crows and gulls hour"

footnotes and fancy free, eye to the anvilled hot iron glow
the hour that I first believed, the day of lithogenesis

one can see the galleries which surround the keep
the hour of lattices, the fourth hour of landmarks and mines

there is now a system of particles, and the first effect of snow
the ill-fated hour, the elapsed moment of the mating wheel

in your insane search to overcome the Devil
the hour approaches with great steps

arriving well before hostilities, I have time to discover places
I have hours before the tour of the salt trees

I have hours before the tour.

Ways of Shining, Ways of Burning

They lived along bloomed banks
with that green that overflows the doors
in the beautiful city of witches.

He was a painter nailing his tables,
hers was the face of the invading mirror;
she countenanced the vivid sea, he framed the fraudulent
    light.

They did their marriage, they believed their performance,
an old, an imperishable melody.
They believed in world speed, machines, and the modern
    city.
They believed in God while they bounced toward the horizon.

Which sea does not have a storm?
At times they were nothing but horse outpanting horse;
at times they sulked with hunger with mad tongues
twisting in one hundred ways.

In their laughter, the dynamic arabesques
of soot and stars, of convicted crows:
the stunned air shuddered on their skin.

They are buried in hollow sand,
in the place of their beautiful crimes.

ABOUT THE AUTHOR

—

Steven Laird is a full time technical editor for a Toronto human resources consulting firm. His poetry has appeared in many Canadian journals, including *Descant, Event, The New Quarterly, The Fiddlehead* and *Grain,* while his reviews, interviews and essays have appeared in *Books in Canada, The Canadian Writers Journal,* and online at *Writers Block* and *BookNinja.* A Toronto native, he is also a former resident of both Fredericton (in 1984 he was awarded the New Brunswick Writers Federation's poetry prize) and St. John's (where he served on the board of the Writers Alliance of Newfoundland and Labrador). Steven is now at work on an anthology of very short Canadian poems, planning an anthology of collage poetry, and compiling a second collection of his own poetry.

MEMBRE DE SCABRINI MEDIA

Québec, Canada
2005